MANAGING YOUR BAND

Scott Witmer

VISIT US AT

WWW.ABDOPUBLISHING.COM

Published by ABDO Publishing Company, 8000 West 78th Street, Suite 310, Edina, MN 55439.
Copyright ©2010 by Abdo Consulting Group, Inc. International copyrights reserved in all countries.
No part of this book may be reproduced in any form without written permission from the publisher.
ABDO & Daughters™ is a trademark and logo of ABDO Publishing Company.

Printed in the United States.

PRINTED ON RECYCLED PAPER

Editor & Graphic Design: John Hamilton
Cover Design: John Hamilton
Cover Photo: iStockphoto
Interior Photos and Illustrations: Digidesign-pg 14; Getty Images-pgs 6, 7, 8, 9, 10, 11, 12, 13, 15, 16, 17, 19, 21, 22, 23, 28; iStockphoto-pgs 1, 3, 4, 5, 20, 25, 26, 27, 29; Jupiter Images-pg 18; Nicole Atkins & The Black Sea-pg 24.

Library of Congress Cataloging-in-Publication Data

Witmer, Scott.
  Managing your band / Scott Witmer.
      p. cm. -- (Rock band)
  Includes index.
  ISBN 978-1-60453-693-5
  1. Rock music--Vocational guidance--Juvenile literature. I. Title.
  ML3795.W526 2009
  781.66068--dc22
                                        2009006610

CONTENTS

STARTING YOUR BAND

Rock Band—everyone knows the term. It brings to mind a group of people playing guitars and drums on a stage, with a wild audience below them, singing along and cheering for more. But what exactly is the definition of a band? The dictionary defines band as "a group of persons, animals, or things; especially: a group of musicians organized for ensemble playing."

Traditionally, a rock band consists of at least three people. Two musicians are called a duo. One musician is called a solo act. Yet you never hear the term "rock duo," or "rock solo act." In rock and roll, the term band is very loosely used. There are solo acts, like Nine Inch Nails, that are widely referred to as a band. Hall and Oates were considered a band, even though they were a duo. So, when forming a rock band, the number of musicians isn't as important as the music they play.

Most rock bands have at least three members.

The number of musicians in a band isn't
as important as the music they play.

Once you've decided to start a rock band, where is the best place to recruit members? There are no simple answers to that question. The stories of how famous rock bands got together are as many and diverse as the music they play. Bands have been formed by friends, by answering ads in the newspapers or online, or by introductions from mutual acquaintances. No matter where you meet potential bandmates, there are several guidelines you should follow.

Members of a band should get along with each other. Bandmates spend countless hours writing, rehearsing, recording, and performing, not to mention possibly spending hours together in a cramped tour bus. To enjoy your time in a rock band, it's probably a good idea to enjoy the people in the band with you.

Of course, there are many stories of famous band members and their notorious disputes. Axl Rose and Slash of Guns N' Roses, Noel and Liam Gallagher of Oasis, and the members of The Eagles have all had personal differences of one kind or another. However, the important thing to remember is that these bandmates were all friends when they started out.

Liam (left) and Noel (right) Gallagher of Oasis.

Lead singer Bono (left) and guitarist The Edge (right) of U2.

While diverse musical tastes and inspiration can be good for a band, it can also tear a band apart. Band members should have similar musical influences, and not differ too wildly on what type of music they want to perform. A country music guitarist is not usually a good match for a techno-synth band.

After your bandmates are all assembled, it is time to name your band. Again, there are several memorable stories from the history of rock about how famous band names were created. There are no rules on naming your band, but it should be something that all your bandmates agree upon. Picture your band's name up on a lighted marquee as a test for how well it will work for you. In recent years, bands have been using more and more unconventional names. For example a Sacramento, California, dance-punk band named themselves !!! (pronounced chk chk chk). As long as a band name isn't already taken by another group, and isn't too offensive, it is considered fair game.

Bassist Paul Simonon (right) of The Clash once talked about how the band came up with its name: "It really came to my head when I started reading the newspapers and a word that kept recurring was the word 'clash,' so I said 'The Clash, what about that?' to the others. And they... went for it." The band members liked that the name raised issues of nonconformity and rule-breaking, hallmarks of the punk music movement of the late 1970s and 1980s.

The band named !!! (often pronounced chk chk chk) performing in Sydney, Australia.

PRACTICE SPACES

Finding a good practice space is important to the creation of a new band. Bands can practice anywhere that there is enough space, and where noise complaints will be at a minimum. Newer bands often practice in basements or garages. An entire genre of music, called garage rock, was named for the low-fi recording method that imitates the sound of a garage practice space. It is also fairly common for bands to not have a designated rehearsal space, moving their practice sessions each time they get together. Bands can also rent practice spaces. Some warehouses, or self-storage facilities, will accommodate band practice schedules and allow rock groups to practice there. These spaces usually cost money to rent unless a band member is lucky enough to know the owner.

A self-storage locker or garage can make a great practice space.

Wherever you decide to practice, make sure that it's convenient for all band members.

Regardless of where your physical practice space is, it should meet a few requirements. It should be easily accessible to all band members. Setting a practice space that is many miles away from the drummer will not help the drummer make it to practice regularly. The space should also accommodate the loud noise that will almost certainly occur during practice. Practicing in an apartment building late at night with the guitar amps turned up to 11 will usually result in complaints, if not a visit by the police. Be considerate of people who live near your rehearsal space.

Your practice space should be large enough that your bandmates aren't stepping on each other. There should be enough space to accommodate all of your musical equipment, like drums and guitar amplifiers. Band members should be able to play their instruments easily and have some freedom of movement. It's hard to be creative when you feel like you are trapped in a shoebox. Ideally, the practice space will also be comfortable and relaxing. Your band will spend a lot of time in this space. If it is freezing cold, and has stark white walls with no place to sit, you probably won't enjoy your practice time. The key is to make rehearsal fun, and not feel like work.

Make sure your space is big enough for you to practice with all your energy.

Be considerate of the people who live near your practice space.

13

Technology in recent years has allowed a new type of rehearsal called "ePractice." Band members can each link together over the Internet and share ideas via webcams or software. A fairly successful indie band of the early 2000s, The Postal Service, had members who lived in different parts of the United States. They recorded tracks and mailed them to each other to rehearse and record with. They named their band The Postal Service because of this collaboration method.

There are several computer software programs, such as Apple's GarageBand or Digidesign's Pro Tools, that allow band members to record parts of songs and send them via the Internet to other band members for collaboration. This situation isn't ideal for rehearsing an upcoming live show, but it is very convenient for the songwriting process.

> Screen shots from Digidesign's Pro Tools software.

A good practice space will help you become better performers.

GETTING ALONG

Now that the band has been formed, and a practice space has been found, it's time to play. However, before the band goes too far, it's usually a good idea to lay down some basic ground rules. These rules can be as simple as "no drugs or alcohol," or it can include an elaborate multi-page list of goals and guidelines.

When working with other people, there will almost certainly be disputes. It is a good practice to have a dispute resolution plan in place before the disagreement happens. Then all disputes can be quickly and fairly resolved. If the band has more than two members, a vote among all members is usually the best method. Some bands resolve disputes with a simple coin toss, or rock-paper-scissors. One media company in Minnesota has a clause in its bylaws that settles deadlocked disputes by kickboxing! This is not recommended. Disputes between members should be settled quickly, since lingering disagreements can hurt a band's rehearsals, writing process, and performances.

> Creativity and great performances result when everyone in the band feels that they're being treated fairly and with respect.

Disputes almost always arise when working with other people. The key is to resolve disagreements quickly and fairly.

Another area that should be talked about is the division of labor. There is actual work that needs to be done in a band, and that work should be divided equally. Figure out ahead of time who will be responsible for

Being in a band means working with people who have their own ideas.

each task, and assign them accordingly. For example, band members interested in graphic design should be put in charge of promotional posters and other graphic arts tasks. A band member with a van could be responsible for driving to gigs. The division of labor should be equal, fair, and agreed upon by everyone. There's nothing worse than watching your drummer talk to fans after a gig while you're carrying instruments out to the van.

When you choose to join a band, keep in mind that you're joining other people who have their own ideas. Merging these different ideas can definitely stimulate creativity. However, when creative differences arise, try to see your bandmates' points of view. Sometimes, accepting someone else's opinion, even if it's different from your own, will yield amazing results. If the drummer isn't playing exactly what you imagined when you wrote your song, give it a chance.

Being in a band isn't about one person having complete creative control. It's about a collaborative creative process. Giving up some control will make your band more relaxed, creative, and fun. If your goal is to have complete control of every aspect of the creative process, then maybe being in a band isn't for you. Remember, a band is a group of individuals working together.

A fair division of labor can be as simple as deciding who brings the snacks, and who drives the van.

PROMOTION

When a band is ready to perform, the next step is promotion. Promotion is important to getting the word out about a new band. The goal is to generate "buzz" about your band, and convince people to attend performances or purchase a CD.

Big-name acts have entire public relations firms that focus on promoting the band. New bands must often handle this task themselves. The best promotion is designed to reach as many people as possible. A good place to start is your band's circle of influence, your friends and family. Contacting all the people that the band members know to inform them of an upcoming show is very effective. Everyone likes to support their friends and family, and yours will most likely want to support you and your band.

Email is very effective. Keep a list of email addresses of everyone you know, and regularly send out updates on your band's upcoming concerts. All of your friends can very easily forward your email notice to all of *their* friends, and so on. When you send an email to 50 friends, it could theoretically hit thousands of email inboxes. A helpful idea is to send two emails—one to announce the show, and a follow-up email a few days before the date of your concert. This serves as a helpful reminder to friends who may have either forgotten about your upcoming show, or hadn't originally been able to attend.

Billy Joe Armstrong of Green Day performing at the Shoreline Amphitheater in Mountain View, California. Established bands like Green Day hire companies that handle promotions, but bands just starting out must do the work themselves.

A popular form of rock band promotion is the concert poster. Concert posters, or flyers, are a single-sheet advertisement for a band's upcoming performance. They should contain the name of the band, and the date and location of the concert. The best concert posters catch the eye of the public, and generate interest in the band. There are several concert posters

Posters and flyers are a very effective way to promote your band.

that have become legendary, such as the posters for 1960s rock legends The Grateful Dead and The Jimi Hendrix Experience.

Many bands enlist the services of professional artists to create amazing flyers that can be considered works of art. In fact, there are several published books that document the history of rock posters, showcasing memorable examples from many decades.

Concert posters are most often hung in music venues, especially the venue for an upcoming performance. They are also placed anywhere that public notices can be legally hung, like public telephone poles, school notice boards, or inside business windows (with permission, of course). They can also be distributed by hand on the street. The more posters and advertisements you get out into the public, the more interest will be generated for your show.

THE JIMI HENDRIX EXPERIENCE "FLYING EYEBALL" POSTER

In recent years, the Internet has been used with great success by new bands. Perhaps the most important promotion tool a band can use is a web site. A well-designed web site can inform fans about upcoming shows, offer a band's music for download and sampling, and display and sell merchandise. A web site can also provide other extras, such as posting pictures, blogs, and information about the band.

Web sites can be created in a variety of ways. If you have very little computer experience, you can pay a company to design and maintain your web site. But if you don't have much money, like most start-up bands, there are other options that can fit your budget. There are several "do-it-yourself" web sites available on the Internet. Free social networking sites, like MySpace and Facebook, have exposed bands to thousands of new fans. These web sites allow new bands to post their songs and band info for free, and then link to their friend's profiles. The more friends they have, the bigger the circle of promotion they can generate. In fact, record companies have recently begun searching for bands on these web sites, and can gauge how popular a band is based on how many friends or hits the band page has. There are also several independent music web sites that feature unsigned bands, with the hope of giving them needed exposure.

A Myspace page for alternative rock band Nicole Atkins & the Black Sea.

Blogs are another excellent source of promotion. Bands that maintain regularly updated blogs can maximize exposure by letting fans know about upcoming shows. Blogs allow a band's audience to connect with the musicians on a very personal level.

Web sites and blogs have become extremely popular in recent years as a way for bands to gain more exposure to fans while maintaining a personal relationship with their audience. Check out what is available, and get your band's information on as many Internet sites as possible. The more places your band's info is available, the greater the chance that potential fans can find you.

Maintaining a regularly updated blog is a great way to stay connected with your fans.

ADVANCED MANAGEMENT

When bands get bigger and more popular, they may want to delegate some of their responsibilities to a manager. A manager is a professional who specializes in aspects of the music business other than the writing and performing. The band members are then free to concentrate on writing, recording, and playing gigs, which is probably why they started a band in the first place. A manager can help the band with bookings and booking agents, promotions, and contract negotiations with record labels and recording studios.

A manager's job is to further a band's career, and help guide them with professional decisions. A manager also coordinates a band's promotional activities. He or she is responsible for scheduling performances, promo appearances, and rehearsals. The manager is also responsible for making sure that the band shows up on time to scheduled appearances. Some managers are also in charge of finances until the band is big enough to hire a dedicated business manager or accountant. A manager usually is paid a commission, or part of the band's income from concerts and album sales.

> Having a manager frees bands to do what they do best: create and perform great music.

> Established bands often hire managers, or even teams of professionals, to help them with their business management.

When bands reach the "big time" and get signed to a record label, the duties of promotion are passed on to a public relations team, or PR manager. Most often, the first thing that the PR manager is responsible for is building a street team. These are organizations of people whose only job is promoting the band in public. These teams are usually made up of young volunteers who are fans of the band. Street teams take over the tasks of hanging flyers and stickers, and spreading word-of-mouth about the band. They usually talk about the band to friends and acquaintances, and convince them to buy the band's albums or come to their concerts. Street team members also may link their social web sites to the band's web site, giving the band more online exposure. Basically, a street team is a group of fans with the sole purpose of doing whatever they can to recruit more fans for the band. The record label pays for these activities, but the street team members themselves are not usually paid.

Most record labels have large financial resources, and can afford to pay out more money to promote a band. The promotion that a record label can provide can include widespread advertising, like radio, television, and billboard spots. A record-label PR manager can also arrange for a band to appear on local radio shows to promote albums. The goal of record label promotion is to blitz the media with as much information, or "buzz," about a band as possible. If more people become interested in a band, then more people will buy the band's newest album. And increased record sales are the ultimate goal of both the record label and the artists.

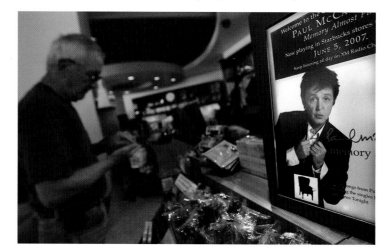

 A Starbucks Coffee promotion of a new Paul McCartney album.

When a public relations manager creates "buzz" about a band, it results in more ticket sales.

GLOSSARY

BLOG

A type of web site that is frequently updated, similar to a diary that is posted online. Blogs are excellent ways for bands to keep in touch with their fans.

BOOKING AGENT

An employee of a band or venue who arranges concert dates. Usually, only established bands can afford booking agents. Bands that are just starting out must learn how to arrange gigs on their own.

BUZZ

Word-of-mouth discussions about your band. If your performances generate a lot of positive buzz, your audiences will almost certainly grow.

ENSEMBLE

A group of musicians, actors, or dancers who perform together.

GIG

A job as a musician, often a live performance.

GRAPHIC DESIGN

Also called graphic arts, the skill of combining photos, illustrations, and type on a printed page or web site in order to tell a story or sell a product in the most effective way possible. Good graphic design catches the eye, is entertaining, and reinforces the message. A striking, consistent graphic design on flyers, posters, web pages, and other materials will help startup bands establish their "look," or identity.

PR

An abbreviation for "public relations." Companies and other organizations, like bands, use PR to keep a good image with the public. A PR manager can keep a band in the public eye by using advertising, such as radio, television, or posters. A PR manager can also arrange to have a band appear at media interviews or events to promote their music.

PROMOTION

An advertising tool that publicizes a band, making the public aware of its existence, the kind of music it plays, and upcoming concerts.

RECORD LABEL

A company that manages, produces, markets, and distributes music and music videos by various bands. The "label" in the name refers to the days when music was mainly recorded on vinyl disks. The company's logo, plus song information, was printed on a circular sticker placed in the center of the record.

RECORDING STUDIO

A place for recording sounds, such as music or the spoken word. Usually, a recording studio is divided into two or more rooms. The "studio" is the place where a person or group goes to speak, play, or sing. The "control room" holds most of the technical recording equipment. A recording studio may also have one or more "isolation booths," which are rooms where artists playing louder instruments, such as drums, are recorded separately. By keeping loud instruments separate, their sound doesn't mingle with that of the other artists. This makes for a cleaner recording.

VENUE

The place where a concert is performed.

INDEX